Perfect Patios & Terraces

Andrew Mikolajski

HERMES
HOUSE

This edition is published by Hermes House, an imprint of Anness Publishing Ltd
Hermes House, 88–89 Blackfriars Road, London SE1 8HA
tel. 020 7401 2077; fax 020 7633 9499
vwww.hermeshouse.com; www.annesspublishing.com

If you like the images in this book and would like to investigate using them for
publishing, promotions or advertising, please visit our website
www.practicalpictures.com for more information.

Publisher: Joanna Lorenz
Managing Editor: Helen Sudell
Series Designer: Larraine Shamwana
Designer: Andrew Heath

ETHICAL TRADING POLICY
Because of our ongoing ecological investment programme, you, as our customer, can have
the pleasure and reassurance of knowing that a tree is being cultivated on your behalf to
naturally replace the materials used to make the book you are holding. For further
information about this scheme, go to www.annesspublishing.com/trees

A CIP catalogue record for this book is available from the British Library.

PERFECT
PATIOS
& TERRACES

ADD AN EXTRA DIMENSION TO YOUR HOME
WITH AN OUTDOOR ROOM

Andrew Mikolajski

CONTENTS

Introduction

IF GARDEN BEDS AND BORDERS EXIST FOR PLANTS, A PATIO OR TERRACE IS CONCEIVED WITH PEOPLE IN MIND. THIS IS A DYNAMIC PART OF THE GARDEN, AND THE STYLE WE SET HERE IS A REFLECTION OF OUR LIFESTYLE AS MUCH AS OF OUR SKILL AS GARDENERS.

WHAT IS A PATIO?

A garden designer might refer to the patio or terrace as an interface. Traditionally, it is the area that links the house with the garden, though in an urban setting the patio may constitute the whole of the outdoor space.

Whatever the size of the garden, the patio shares some aspects of both the indoor and the outdoor environment. Increasingly people think of such an area as an extension of the house. Paving or decking, tables and chairs, awnings and even heaters mean that it can function like an additional room,

Above: A charming, well-furnished terrace invites you to step out of the house for morning coffee, afternoon tea or alfresco meals on summer evenings.

an extra living space that is especially suitable for entertaining, eating and relaxing. But it can also be the setting for the garden's most spectacular and precious plants.

The patio now merits (and receives) as much care and thought when it comes to selecting materials and furnishings – its style, in other words – as we give to sitting rooms, bedrooms, kitchens and bathrooms.

FROM HOUSE TO GARDEN

Ideally, there should be a smooth transition from house to garden. Many people harbour the image of a beautiful house with full-length windows flung wide open and leading on to a spacious terrace which, in turn, overlooks a manicured lawn and an immaculate garden.

Something of that feeling of escape can be created in every garden, even where space is at a premium, but many gardeners have to balance the wish to have a patio or terrace with a desire for a lawn, for a herb or vegetable garden, for beds and borders for flowers and shrubs or for a greenhouse or shed. Except for the smallest courtyards, deciding how much space can be allocated to any or all of the different functions of a garden is part of the planning process, and designing and building the patio must take into account the style of the remainder of the garden, just as its surface and decoration must reflect the interior and exterior style of the house.

Patios and terraces are usually understood as adjoining the house, keeping them warm and sheltered, and within easy reach of the kitchen and other living areas. However, there is no reason why a paved area or deck cannot be created at a distance from the house, linked to it by a path. A large garden might accommodate a second patio, on which could be built a summerhouse or arbour, providing a sheltered place to sit in summer, when you can feel you are in the heart of the country rather than a mere stone's throw from your back door.

Above: A secluded corner is made more appealing by the climbers that clothe and soften the vertical surfaces.

Introduction

ENJOYING YOUR PATIO

Increasingly the patio or terrace has become associated with relaxation, and it should be a peaceful place to unwind and forget the strains of modern living. Food always seems to taste better in the open air, and summer cooking outside is a pleasure even for those who show little enthusiasm in the kitchen. Nowadays, barbecues can be fitted into the smallest spaces and the patio has become a place for dining and entertaining.

Making this space a pleasant, sheltered outdoor room can be achieved by the addition of permanent structures, such as pergolas and screens, or by thoughtful planting, to create shade, colour and fragrance in summer

Above: Choose garden furniture that is in keeping with the style of your terrace. Smart enamelled metal suits the look and scale of a small urban courtyard.

but to allow all the available natural light to reach the windows of the house in winter. A sympathetic choice of materials, and furniture that is both

Above: In a small garden, a simple bench in a sheltered corner will provide a welcome sitting area, especially when it is surrounded by fragrant flowers.

comfortable and appropriate to the patio in size and scale, will increase your enjoyment. Such is the lure of the outdoors that, once you have created your perfect patio, it will be the centre of your home all summer long.

HOW TO USE THIS BOOK

This book is intended to inspire you with fresh ideas and possibilities, but whether you design and build the patio yourself or employ a garden designer and a building contractor, you will still have to define its basic function. The first section, **Planning Considerations**, explores some of the issues you need to consider when you are preparing the design. **Structural Elements** evaluates the relative merits

of the materials that are likely to be at your disposal and the impact they will make, as well as offering hints on how to shelter the area from the elements and to enhance security and privacy. **Patio Planting** describes some suitable plants for the patio.

Choosing a Style discusses some of the styles that are popular in garden design today and suggests how they can be achieved, both through the materials used in construction and through planting. Finally, **Special Features** focuses on those finishing touches that make a patio personal to its owner and that will increase your pleasure in it: choosing the appropriate furniture, lighting and heating the patio, and creating focal points.

Above: Dense planting gives this tiny patio a jungle-like lushness, while the mixed floor materials add an air of informality.

Planning Considerations

There are several issues to consider when you are planning a patio or terrace. Time spent at the early stages is never wasted and will enable you to develop a space you will want to return to again and again.

SITE AND ACCESS

Consider where the patio is to be sited. Easy access from the house is important, and the position of doors leading into the garden may determine your choice. If the patio will be adjacent to the house, will it run the full length of the building? Will it be the same depth throughout or will it have a curved or angled edge to reflect other features in the garden or house?

A patio can also be sited some distance from the house, with a path leading to it, or you might prefer two

Above: *Wooden decking is an ideal material for a patio or terrace where the site is not level.*

or more linked spaces. A concealed area can be especially successful. Imagine a path that disappears among trees or shrubs, leading to a simple, open, paved circle with a single architectural plant or statue at the centre. This kind of feature can make for dynamic contrast and bring an element of surprise into the garden.

A level site poses few problems, but if the ground slopes you need to consider whether you want to construct retaining walls or raised beds so that the patio itself is level and whether you will have to build steps or a ramp so that you can easily and safely get from the patio to the garden.

Make sure that a patio that adjoins the house slopes slightly away from it toward a drain or a border, so that rainwater cannot accumulate near the house wall and cause damp problems.

SIZE MATTERS

Unless it occupies the whole of a small plot, the patio needs to be in scale with the rest of the garden. If it is too small, you are unlikely to make good use of it, but if it is too large, it might look exposed and unwelcoming. If the

Above: *A zigzag path prevents the eye from leaping to the far edge of the patio, tricking you into believing that the space is larger than it is.*

Above: *Plants growing around the patio will soon spill over the edges of paving and steps, but at first you can use containers to soften their hard lines.*

patio has to be large to link two buildings, try breaking up the expanse with changes of level or materials, a raised bed or even a small tree or fountain.

If you are using paving, make sure that the scale of the materials is in pro portion to the overall area. This aspect of the design is often overlooked but will have a significant effect on the success of the area. Big patios are best paved with large slabs, and small with small. In a small area, granite setts are easier on the eye than large slabs, which seem to accentuate the restricted dimensions.

At the planning stage, be sure to allow adequate room for tables and chairs; as well as using them, you will want to walk around them, perhaps serving your guests who are sitting around the table. Make sure there is space for chairs to be pushed back – the

last thing you want is for chairs to topple backward into the neighbouring plants. Leave room for containers and remember that plants in surrounding borders will billow out in summer, further reducing the ground space.

Steps and paths must be wide enough to be safe, and if you need to include handrails or a balustrade, remember to allow for these in your ground plan. The ideal path should be wide enough to allow two people to walk along side by side in comfort, and a width of 2m (6ft) will not seem excessive once plants in adjacent borders have flopped over and softened the edges. If space is really limited, make sure that you will, at least, be able to manoeuvre a lawnmower between the borders or push a wheelbarrow through the garden with ease.

Sun or Shade?

Whether the patio is to be in sun or shade may already be determined by the lie of the house and elements beyond the garden, such as nearby buildings and trees. This is especially likely to be the case in town gardens.

Where you can exercise choice, your future use of the patio may well be influenced by whether it is predominantly in sun or shade and how this varies according to the season and time of day. If the far end of your garden catches the evening sun, you might use and enjoy the spot more if you created a paved area and furnished it with a table and chairs.

Above: If the patio is hot and sunny, there is nothing more refreshing than the sound of bubbling water, as the designer of this feature realized.

The idea of breakfasting on a sunny terrace is particularly appealing, and if you have a patio near the house that gets the morning sun, it is sure to get plenty of use at this time of day. By lunchtime, however, when the sun is much stronger, the same spot may be too hot for comfortable eating.

Often, it is only when the weather is really hot that we remember the need for shade, and although most of us probably dream of long days basking in the sunshine, we are continually reminded about the dangers of over-exposure to ultraviolet light. If the site you have chosen has no natural shade, consider building a pergola over which you could grow deciduous climbers or think about erecting an awning, which can be removed and stored from autumn to spring.

The solid shade cast by a building can make an area too chilly except on the warmest days, but a patio that is overhung by a deciduous tree can be enjoyed on sunny days in spring yet will offer some protection from the sun in summer when the tree is in full leaf. It is pleasant to relax with a drink on a patio or deck that is warmed by the evening sun, even if this was in shade during most of the day.

WINDY SITES

One of the worst problems to beset gardeners is swirling wind. Most small, enclosed gardens are unaffected by this problem, but if the site is relatively open, strong gusts can mar your enjoyment at any time of year. A long, narrow garden flanked by tall walls or fences may suffer from the wind-tunnel effect. You can shelter a patio with a fence, or with trees and shrubs. If you choose the latter, plant deciduous species, because they tend to filter the wind; dense evergreens can help to create even stronger currents.

On the other hand, if the patio is to do double duty as a utility space for drying washing, a certain amount of wind can only be an advantage.

Above: Planting up to the edge of the paved area is the best way of linking this shady patio with the rest of the garden.

Above: A well-maintained hedge is not only attractive but also affords maximum privacy and shelter from gusting wind.

Planning Considerations

CHILDREN

If there are children in the family, they will enjoy having a smooth, level patio to play on, but safety issues are paramount. Although bumps and falls are part of growing up, concrete surfaces and raised areas with no guard rails pose particular hazards. Instead of concrete or paving slabs, consider using softer materials, such as decking, bark chippings or even the rubberized tiles that are used in public play areas.

Open water should be avoided altogether in gardens where small children play. If you must have a water feature, install a small bubble fountain over cobbles, or a wall-mounted spout, and sink the reservoir into the ground.

ELDERLY AND DISABLED GARDENERS

Ease of access is a vital consideration for anyone with restricted mobility. If the garden falls steeply away from the house, rather than terracing the patio, create instead a gentle slope that can be navigated from level to level by wheelchair users. If you can install a raised bed, perhaps with a hand rail, along one side of the slope, so much the better: it will help to prevent falls and other mishaps, besides bringing any plants within reach of the gardener.

Surface materials require special consideration, too. If you opt for paving, it should be laid smoothly, with no proud edges that can trip any

Above: A well-built sandpit in a warm corner can make for hours of creative play.

Above: Raised beds surrounding a perfectly even paved surface make this patio the ideal outdoor space for a disabled or elderly gardener.

Above: Decking squares are easy to lay, and are available with a ridged surface that gives a safer footing for the very young and old than plain, smooth wood.

gardeners who are not absolutely stable on their feet. Some smooth concrete surfaces can be slippery when wet, so either roughen the surface with aggregate to prevent slips and falls or use some other material that is already rough. Grooved or ridged decking provides a better grip underfoot than plain wood and can also be laid in attractive patterns.

Older gardeners will want to avoid surfaces that are going to require constant attention and maintenance. Even paving slabs will attract moss and lichens in time (the first sign is a greenish tinge, usually around the edges) and will need to be treated. Special products are available that have to be sprayed or watered on; alternatively, the lichen has to be removed the hard way, with water and a wire brush. Softwood decking is

easy to lay, but unless it is tanalized (pressure treated) it will require regular applications of preservative.

FAMILY PETS

Cats and dogs will adore basking in the sun on smooth, warm paving stones. Extensive areas of fine gravel are best avoided if you or your neighbours have cats, which are likely to see it as a large and convenient litter tray. Chemical deterrents are available, but their effect is temporary. If you are troubled by visiting cats, it may be worth investing in sound- or motion-activated deterrents, which either emit a high-pitched whistle or spray intruders with water.

Male dogs regard almost anything as a potential urinal, and even the best-trained and exercised animals have accidents sometimes, so keep some disinfectant handy.

13

SPRINGING A SURPRISE

Although most patios and terraces will be fairly open spaces in the garden you can still introduce an element of surprise. If you have a large garden, with a patio adjoining the house, you may wish to close up the far side by means of a fence or wall so that the rest of the garden is virtually hidden, and perhaps accessible only through a gate. In this way, the patio itself becomes almost literally an outdoor room. A less extreme feeling of separation can be created by dense planting to either side of a path leading away from the patio. If the path turns a corner and disappears out of sight, the invitation to explore the garden will be well-nigh irresistible.

In a large garden, an alternative effect can be achieved by siting a patio some distance from the house and screening it, either by tall planting or by a wall or fence, so that you seem to alight on it as if by accident; the presence of a seat will encourage you to linger there. Ideally, to increase the illusion that you have really made an escape, the house should not be visible from the patio, but if this is not possible, arrange any seating to face away from the house – instead directing the eye to a pool, a statue or an especially fine architectural plant.

RELAXING AND ENTERTAINING

If you like to entertain a lot and to dine alfresco, you need to allow ample room for a table and chairs. Bear in mind that people will want to push their chairs back from the table without falling into the borders, and to be able to walk around behind them. If the table is in a sunny position, you'll

Above: Use paint to alter the atmosphere of a corner of your patio. You can easily change the colour if you tire of the effect.

Above: In a large garden you can create an element of surprise with winding paths and gateways to secret enclosed areas.

need to provide shade in the middle of the day. Choose a large parasol, or one that you can set at an angle, so that it shades your guests as well as the food on the table.

You might want to consider building an integral barbecue into the patio wall, but these days transportable models, which can be stored in a utility room or garage when not in use, are widely available and are not too costly. Whichever type of barbecue you prefer, safety considerations should make sure it can be used well away from any potentially flammable materials, including overhanging plants. You'll also need a level surface nearby where you can rest plates.

Privacy will be an issue for most people, especially town-dwellers. If you use the patio for sunbathing, you will probably welcome shelter from

Above: If your table is sited in the middle of a sunny terrace, a large parasol is an essential accessory in summer.

prying eyes, possibly in the form of a fence or trees, but make sure that the shadow is not cast on the patio itself or you will be defeating the object.

Above: Colourful balls signpost the path to a second paved area, tucked away out of sight of the rest of the garden.

15

Structural Elements

THERE IS A WIDE RANGE OF MATERIALS THAT CAN BE USED TO CREATE A PATIO OR TERRACE, AND SOME OF THE MOST POPULAR ARE DISCUSSED HERE, TOGETHER WITH SOME SUGGESTIONS ON HOW TO SCREEN THE AREA AND WHICH PLANTS ARE MOST SUITABLE.

CHOOSING THE SURFACE

The siting and size of your patio will both influence your choice of surface material, but there are several other factors to consider, including cost, ease of laying, maintenance and appearance. The style needs to be appropriate to its setting, and if you have an old property, reclamation yards are a good source of suitable materials.

Above: Restraint is the keynote of this modern, elegant decked area.

Decking

As an alternative to paving, the use of wooden decking is now well established. It is a natural choice in areas where wood is in abundance and the climate is relatively dry and sunny. Its nature makes it ideal for strong, geometric designs and it ages sympathetically. Decks are ideal if you need to make a raised platform over sloping ground, and a rail around the deck will enhance the colonial feel.

Decking is laid on a framework of timber joists, in the same way as a traditional interior wooden floor. The joists are themselves supported on pillars, and the sides of the decking are usually covered with facing boards to conceal the space beneath.

You can customize decking by painting or staining it, but whatever finish you choose will fade with age so you may need to repeat the treatment every year or so. The better quality the wood, the better it ages. Hardwood is more resistant to decay than softwood, but if economy dictates that you must use softwood, make sure it has been tanalized (pressure treated) for longer life.

Above: Slabs and gravel are common enough building materials but can still have distinction if used with discretion.

Apart from traditional boards, decking is widely available in the form of square wooden tiles, which can be laid in geometric patterns to add interest to the surface. A grooved finish will provide a safer walking surface than smooth wood in damp weather.

Stone

Natural stone is beautiful to look at but is expensive and usually heavy to handle and difficult to lay, especially if the individual stones are of different thicknesses. Some stones break up easily and cannot be recommended for paving. Make sure you find a good match with the local stone, especially where this has been used as a building material.

Concrete and Artificial Stone

One of the most versatile of all building materials, concrete has become a fashionable alternative to paving, as new laying and colouring techniques give it a fresh style. You can either accept it for what it is and opt for a great sweep of unadorned concrete – perfect in a high-tech or minimalist garden – or you can use it in one of its less immediately obvious forms, as slabs, which look to all intents and purposes like natural stone and are available in a variety of shapes, colours and textures. Good-quality concrete slabs are a good imitation of real stone and are much cheaper and easy to lay.

You can make your own paving slabs from concrete, which you can tint to the exact colour you want. Either make individual slabs in a mould or just lay the concrete and groove the surface before it is fully set to suggest paving slabs (for this you will need a keen eye and a steady hand).

PATIO PLANNING AND BUILDING BASICS

• When a patio is built to adjoin the house, make sure that the final surface of the patio is not higher than the damp-proof (water-proof) course.

• Lay paving stones or concrete so that the patio slopes very slightly away from the house wall toward a drain or border, to prevent puddles forming. The drop should be about 16mm per metre ($^5/_8$in per yard).

• If you have to include steps in your design to cope with changes of level, define the edges clearly with contrasting materials.

COMBINING ELEMENTS

While you might initially decide it is a good idea to stick to a single building material to keep a patio or terrace looking smart and uncluttered, it can be effective to combine different elements. In fact, it makes sense to do so. Think about how you decorate indoors: a sitting room, for instance, combines a number of textures – carpets, heavy-duty furnishing fabrics, sheer curtains – and a bathroom can unite chrome with ceramic tiling and mirrors or warm cork tiles.

If your patio is a large one, using more than one material for the surface can help to break up an expanse that

Above: A mixture of large stones and cobbles creates a natural-looking area, enhanced by informal planting and the trickle of water from a bubble fountain.

might otherwise start to seem bleak. It can also help to define different parts of the patio, such as the area around the table, or the children's play area.

Combining materials is also a good way of introducing small quantities of desirable but expensive elements into the design. A small mosaic motif or an edging strip of expensive tiles can be incorporated with more workaday materials to provide interest and focus. Alternatively, introduce areas of cobbles set in concrete. Decking

Above: This clever use of different materials, textures and colours helps define discrete areas of the patio. The gravel softens the hard edges of the bricks.

cast light shade might be appropriate on a large patio or a specimen shrub on a smaller one. This can also be an excellent way of creating a herb garden close to the house, so that you do not need to walk far from the kitchen every time you want to pick a handful of fresh herbs for garnish or flavour. The paving will also help to contain rampant herbs such as mint.

If you have opted for gravel laid over a membrane spread directly on garden soil, a few judiciously pierced holes will allow for planting. You need to choose the plants carefully, however, because some species will actually seed themselves in the gravel and can push their roots through the membrane if this is water-permeable.

works surprisingly well with gravel, but you should be careful when combining decking squares with concrete slabs. If they are of roughly the same size, the eye gets confused and will "jump" from one to the other, which can be unsettling and discomfiting.

Water and decking work well together to create a seaside feel. An expanse of water is cooling, but where space is limited or the presence of young children rules out a pool, a vertical water feature incorporating a spout or a small bubble fountain might be considered.

In a paved area you might like to miss out a few slabs here and there to allow for planting – a tree that will

Above: In spring, brilliant blue grape hyacinths (Muscari) will happily push their way through gravel.

Above: Brick (block) paving weathers gracefully and looks wonderful when colonized by small plants and mosses.

Brick

If your house is built of bricks (blocks), it is usually easy to find a good match for use on the patio. House bricks, whether new or reclaimed, are, however, not the best type to use as paving: they are not frostproof and tend to crack and crumble in extreme weather. For durability, look for the highest specification. Facing and engineering bricks are frost-resistant.

Bricks are eminently suitable for patterned paving. They can be laid in a variety of bonds, much as walls are built, and are also suitable for herringbone or basketweave effects.

Tiles

Terracotta tiles are beautiful, and make it possible to use the same style of flooring outdoors as you have used in the kitchen, but they are less durable than other types so are best used under cover, perhaps for a covered loggia or summerhouse. Pottery roofing tiles can be used laid on edge, either on their own or in conjunction with other materials, as a large quantity is needed to cover the ground.

Cobbles and Setts

If you can find a source – usually a reclamation yard – old street cobbles and setts are attractive, but they are not always easy to walk on, and any seating placed on cobbles will be distinctly unstable. They are best used to break up larger areas of paving, either in the form of a strip to demarcate separate areas or to highlight an edge or as decoration, in the form of swirls and spirals.

Above: Bright tiles in a formal pool are elegantly set off by a terracotta edging.

Gravel

Easy to lay and to maintain, gravel is an ideal surface material. It can be laid direct on compacted earth, ideally over a weed-suppressing membrane, or on top of another hard surface. It is available in a range of grades and colours, and it has the additional advantage of combining well with other hard surfaces. It is very useful for filling awkward corners and curved areas. The main drawbacks are that it must be contained by edging if it is not to travel, both around the garden and into the house on the soles of shoes, and it is irresistible to cats.

Railway Sleepers

Available from reclamation yards and some specialist garden suppliers, railway sleepers (ties) are usually used for edging raised beds, as low walls or as steps. Sleepers are heavy and when they are used in a single row they usually need no fixing. However, if they are used as steps or to create a raised bed several sleepers high, when there will be a considerable weight of soil behind them, they should be held together with brackets.

Sleepers can be laid directly on the ground, but if they are impregnated with preservative, lay them on plastic sheeting and line the inside with plastic to prevent the tar from leaching into the soil and harming the plants. If possible, buy untreated sleepers.

Above: Smooth stones and pea shingle look attractive but are best used as decorative details as they may not be easy to walk on.

Mosaics

If you are naturally creative – or have a good friend who is – you can enliven any outdoor space with a mosaic that will give pleasure throughout the year. Mosaics work especially well near water – a reminder of the Islamic concept of the paradise garden, even though your principal source of inspiration may lie elsewhere.

Experiment with patterns of broken tiles or coloured stones, even sea shells, in a dry mix of sand and cement. Once you are satisfied with the design, sprinkle with water to set the mortar or simply allow soil moisture to be drawn up by capillary action, which will do the job for you. Mosaics tend to be less durable than other forms of paving, so restrict their use to areas that will not be subjected to heavy traffic or use them to make small patterns or decorative motifs.

WALLS AND FENCES

At the most basic level, walls and fences mark the boundaries between neighbouring gardens. The need for privacy is often important, particularly in a small town garden, and a solid wall or fence will provide maximum security and privacy.

Within the garden, however, these structures may have different functions. They can be used to divide separate areas and levels or to provide shelter, and when a new patio is being designed, you may want to erect additional fences or walls at the same time.

If a windbreak is required, for example, a trellis fence will filter the strongest winds better than a solid wall. A compromise can be achieved by topping a low fence or wall with trellis panels. If you want to preserve a lovely view from the terrace, a low fence may be adequate shelter for small plants.

Walls

A new garden wall is a luxury few can afford these days owing to high labour costs, and there are, in any case, often local regulations governing the height of solid boundaries, so if you already have a wall, make the most of it.

Within a garden, however, as long as you have space to dig out the footings, walls can be used either to enhance the privacy of a patio or to create secret places and hidden corners. A wall up to 1m (3ft) tall can be built by anyone with the relevant skills, but seek professional help with anything higher.

A wall to edge a patio can be built of a material that matches the house and patio floor itself. Brick and stone are obvious choices, but concrete can be incredibly stylish, especially if the house is a modern one, and the material lends itself to abstract and innovative designs. Glass blocks are excellent in a contemporary design, and are extremely attractive in association with water features.

Brick, glass and concrete can also be used to make curved structures, but the weight and the techniques involved suggest that their construction is best left in the hands of professional contractors.

Above: *Use wall-baskets and hanging baskets to bring colour to plain walls.*

Above: Unusually patterned stones make an idiosyncratic boundary wall. Planting softens the effect, preventing it from becoming overpowering.

Above: Basketweave fencing is a sympathetic background for plants and is easy to erect. It requires regular varnishing to lengthen its life.

Fences

Most fencing is made of softwood, and ready-made panel fences are easy to erect, popular and effective. As a rule, the more expensive the fencing, the better the quality and the longer it is likely to last. Wherever possible, use tanalized (pressure-treated) wood to ensure a long life.

When you are using a fence within the garden to create a shelter around a patio, consider it from both points of view. For example, a fence around the edge of a sitting area might prevent you from seeing the compost heap, but if the patio is next to the house it might also pose a security problem: you might not be able to see the back of your house when you are working elsewhere in the garden.

When you are choosing fence panels, look at how they have been made. Close-board fences, made of upright timbers, look good in a woodland garden and anywhere where you want to emphasize verticals. Interwoven fences tend to stress horizontal lines and are useful when you want to exaggerate the depth of the garden. In an Oriental-style setting, a bamboo fence is entirely appropriate, but it can be too lightweight for use anywhere other than in a sheltered corner. Trellis has the advantage that it functions well as a windbreak but can be clothed with dense climbers in summer to provide maximum privacy.

All fences can be painted or stained, either to soften their impact or to help them blend in with their surroundings. Alternatively, you might want to make a strong colour statement by painting them so that they really stand out. Whatever you do, make sure that any preservative or paint you use on the fences is plant friendly.

HEDGES

A hedge can be planted either to give privacy or to mark off one part of the garden from another. Thorny hedges, such as pyracantha, can also offer increased security if they are used around the boundary, but they are not ideal near children's play areas or beside paths and sitting areas.

Deciduous or Evergreen?

If you just want a windbreak, a deciduous hedge would be a good choice, because the bare branches will filter strong winter winds but in summer the leaf cover will provide shade and help to minimize noise. For an evergreen barrier, conifers such as yew (*Taxus*), box (*Buxus*) and *Thuja* are

*Above: Traditional and still best, tightly clipped box (*Buxus*) is a splendid choice for low hedging to surround beds in a formal garden.*

traditional choices, but they need regular clipping for a sheer surface and to restrict the height.

Do not plant Leyland cypress (× *Cuprocyparis leylandii*) within the garden: it will take the nutrients from other plants and will need to be clipped three or four times a year to prevent it from taking over completely.

Bear in mind that evergreens tend to be less tolerant of urban pollution. This is an important factor in a town garden, hence the popularity of privet (*Ligustrum*), which shows outstanding resistance.

Informal Hedges

In a town or Oriental-style garden, bamboos can make an elegant screen, and the light rustle of their leaves in summer is an added delight. Make sure you choose carefully: some species are invasive, and it is a sensible precaution to restrict the root system wherever they are planted. Plant them in large tubs and sink these into the ground or surround the roots with paving slabs buried vertically.

Climbing and rambling roses make good barriers and have the bonus of summer flowers and fragrance. Alternatively, an informal evergreen hedge can be created with Portugal laurel (*Prunus lusitanica*) or spotted laurel

HEDGING PLANTS FOR PATIOS
Aucuba
Berberis
Buxus
Cotoneaster
Escallonia
Euonymus
Fagus
Fuchsia
Griselinia
Ilex
Laurus
Lonicera nitida
Prunus (evergreen)
Rosa (some)
Rosmarinus
Santolina

(*Aucuba japonica* 'Crotonifolia'), while a mixed hedge of hawthorn (*Crataegus*) and holly (*Ilex*) will suit a country or cottage garden.

Above: *Hollies make good hedges, and berrying forms provide food for birds in winter.* Ilex aquifolium *'J.C. van Tol' has the advantage of almost spineless leaves.*

Above: *The cherry laurel (*Prunus laurocerasus) *makes an excellent informal evergreen hedge. This is the attractive cultivar 'Castlewellan'.*

25

Patio Planting

IN A LARGE GARDEN, THE PLANTING IS DESIGNED TO CONTRIBUTE TO THE OVERALL PICTURE, AND IS OFTEN SEEN FROM A DISTANCE. THE PATIO IS THE PLACE TO GROW SPECIES THAT ARE REWARDING AT CLOSE QUARTERS, SUCH AS THOSE WITH LAVISH FLOWERS OR A HEADY SCENT.

BRINGING THE PATIO TO LIFE

A beautifully designed patio or terrace with pleasing proportions may need only the minimum of plant material to decorate it. The focus of interest may be a beautiful specimen tree, or a pair of elegant containers. Most people who have a garden, however, eventually become hooked on plants, often in spite of themselves, and want to grow more unusual species. It is worth knowing which plants lend themselves especially well to this area of the garden and how they should be grown.

Above: Raised beds, generously planted with miniature roses, will be a source of colour all summer long.

Raised Beds

If you are constructing a completely new patio, you may decide to incorporate raised beds to edge the patio, in place of a balustrade or low wall. On a hard surface they must have in-built weep holes for drainage. Make sure the beds are not so wide that you cannot reach the centre (assuming there is access from both sides); this usually means limiting the width to 1.2m (4ft).

A raised bed has several advantages. It is effectively a large container, which makes it possible to grow plants that would not thrive elsewhere in the garden. Bringing in acid soil, for example, will create a suitable medium for rhododendrons and heathers, which you would not otherwise be able to grow if your soil is alkaline. If the garden soil is poor, raised beds give you the opportunity of importing new soil. Adding grit to improve drainage will open the door to a whole range of alpines and dwarf bulbs.

Combining raised beds with other borders and beds at ground level can bring a certain dynamism to the design, which is especially important if space is restricted.

Above: Ballerina apple trees are ideal patio plants. They can be trained to arch over to make a fruiting bower.

SELECTING PLANTS

What you grow in the ground adjoining the patio is obviously a matter of personal choice. The patio is often quite sheltered and if it is near the house it may benefit from the residual warmth of the walls, allowing you to grow less-hardy species.

If the patio is bounded by walls or fences on one or more sides, the rainfall will be restricted. Either be prepared to water the plants during dry weather or restrict your choice to drought-tolerant species, including bulbs and many herbs.

Planting in Sun

If your patio is sunny, you'll be spoiled for choice when planting up containers for spring and summer colour. Many fruits and vegetables are also extremely decorative, and a surprising number can be grown in containers on the patio. Ballerina apple trees were specially bred for this purpose, but almost any cultivar is suitable provided it has been grafted on to a dwarfing rootstock. Figs thrive in containers against a warm wall, and the root restriction helps produce bigger crops earlier in the plant's life. Luscious strawberries and tomatoes also make attractive plants for a sunny corner, with the bonus that you can pick the ripe fruit from your garden chair.

Above: Well-filled borders and containers soften the severe lines of this simple paved area and create a lush feel.

27

Planting for Shade

If you want the patio to be a shady area for summer relaxation you may have to plant to create shade. Among the many widely available and reliable deciduous trees are ornamental cherries (*Prunus*) and crab apples (*Malus*), which have delightful spring flowers. The best of all shade trees are, perhaps, catalpas and paulownias, both of which have large leaves. Both respond well to pruning so can be planted even where space is limited.

Your patio may already be shaded by walls and trees, but there are plenty of plants that will flourish in cool conditions, and it is easy to create a lush, jungle-like effect with luxurious foliage plants such as hostas and hardy ferns.

Above: This small area has been designed as a cool retreat, with a pool shaded by cleverly supported ivy and a thick wall of luxuriant foliage to create a screen.

Climbers and Ramblers

House walls or fences that abut a patio cry out for the softening effect of climbers. If possible, allow space for small beds between the patio and the wall or fence. Because they are largely woodland plants, most climbers appreciate the cool root run that the paving or decking over their roots will

---

FLOWERS FOR SHADY PATIOS

(a = annual or biennial; p = perennial)
Convallaria majalis p
Dicentra p
Impatiens a
Lobelia a
Pulmonaria p

---

provide. Make sure that such plants receive plenty of water. Your choice of climber will depend on the aspect of the wall: some species revel in the reflected heat; others are happier in shade. Some large-flowered clematis varieties, for instance, will produce flowers of a richer colour when shielded from intense sunlight.

Climbers can also be grown in containers, either placed against a wall or trained on a support that is incorporated in the pot. Some of the weaker-growing or annual climbers are best for containers. Rampant plants, such as wisteria and bougainvillea, can be grown in pots but will need hard pruning to keep them within bounds.

If you want flowering climbers for a confined space, good choices are to be found among the large-flowered hybrid clematis and miniature climb-

> **CLIMBERS FOR PATIOS**
>
> (* = shade tolerant)
> *Bougainvillea* (not hardy*)*
> *Campsis radicans*
> *Clematis* *
> *Hedera* *
> *Humulus lupulus*
> *Hydrangea petiolaris* *
> *Jasminum officinale*
> *Plumbago auriculata* (not hardy*)*
> *Rosa* (miniature climbers*)*
> *Trachelospermum jasminoides*
> *Tropaeolum speciosum*
> *Wisteria*

ing roses. The so-called patio roses and miniature climbers have been specially bred with present needs in mind: they are compact plants that produce an abundance of flowers over a long period. They are ideal for planting in beds, borders and containers. Some of the roses bred for groundcover can also be trained upward, to cover walls and trellises.

Above: Hedera helix *'Buttercup', smaller growing than many ivies, produces its best leaf colour in a sunny position.*

Above: The annual Ipomoea tricolor *has vivid blue flowers and is perfect for guiding over a trellis.*

Above: The poached-egg plant
(Limnanthes douglasii) *is a modest annual that will obligingly seed itself in the cracks of paving and in gravel.*

Perennials and Annuals

Flowering herbaceous plants put the flesh on the bones of the garden, as it were, producing an abundance of greenery and, in most cases, a spectacular show of flowers over a long period. The more compact, sturdy forms are best suited to the patio whereas tall, floppy plants, such as delphiniums and some peonies, which need to be staked, look more effective when planted in the herbaceous border.

Most valuable of all for the patio are the tender perennials, such as felicias, verbenas, pelargoniums and osteospermums, which you can grow from seed or buy as small plants in late spring. These showy plants produce a seemingly unending succession of flowers from the start of summer until the first frosts. They are ideal for all kinds of patio containers, from hanging baskets to large troughs. If you have a greenhouse, plant tender perennials in pots and tubs that can be moved under glass for the winter.

Annuals will also produce flowers all summer, although it is advisable to make both early and late sowings to ensure continuity. Deadhead the plants regularly to encourage them to produce further blooms, and feed them well to maintain their flower power. While perennials and shrubs will give structure to your planting plan, growing annuals allows you to transform the look of your patio with a fresh colour scheme each year.

Above: The succulent-looking evergreen Sedum aizoon *will thrive in the heat reflected by paving.*

Low-growing Shrubs

Compact, tightly growing shrubs are ideal for patios because they are easy to control and naturally stay within bounds. Evergreens that have a pleasing shape, such as Mexican orange blossom (*Choisya ternata*), are obviously desirable, but there are others, such as box (*Buxus*), that can be clipped to shape and some, such as *Phillyrea*, that can be allowed to grow more freely. Small shrubs such as camellia, fuchsia and skimmia can be grown as specimens in containers.

Patio and groundcover roses are recently bred varieties that are quite unlike the often gangly hybrid teas and cluster-flowered roses: they are low-growing, tough and disease-resistant. They smother themselves in flowers and repeat well throughout the summer, making them perfect plants in every way for a sunny patio.

Bulbs and Corms

Many bulbs are ideal patio plants, and not just in containers. Early spring bulbs, such as crocuses and dwarf narcissi, look delightful pushing up through gravel. If you have a hot spot near a sheltering wall, include some of the late-flowering South African species, such as crinums, nerines and *Amaryllis belladonna* (the true amaryllis, not the hippeastrums sold under this name for growing indoors in winter).

SHRUBS FOR PATIOS
Buxus
Calluna
Camellia
Choisya ternata
Conifers (dwarf forms)
Erica
Fuchsia
Hebe
Ilex
Phillyrea
Rhododendron (dwarf forms)
Rosa (patio, miniature and groundcover forms)
Skimmia

BULBS FOR PATIOS
Agapanthus
Amaryllis belladonna
Crinum
Crocus
Dahlia (dwarf forms)
Iris
Lilium
Nerine

Above: *The aptly named pineapple lily (*Eucomis bicolor*) is not quite hardy but will thrive in sheltered conditions.*

Foliage Plants

Delightful as flowers are, they are present for a much shorter period in the plant's annual life cycle than leaves. Leaves are the backdrop to any planting, and once you learn to appreciate their variety of shape, colour and texture, you will come to value them as much as flowers.

Some plants are grown primarily for their foliage. In fact, some of the best – ferns – do not flower at all in the conventional sense. Mainly shade lovers, these are ideal for bringing life to cool, shady, moist corners, perhaps adjoining a basement flat. Team them with hostas for contrast, but watch out for slugs and snails, which also like shady, moist conditions.

Grasses are increasingly popular, and with good reason. They are easy to maintain, and even those that are not evergreen provide a long period of interest, since the old foliage is retained by the plant over winter. A riming of frost on a cold winter's morning only adds to their beauty. They are useful for softening a vivid planting of flowers and work surprisingly well with conifers.

Above: *A cool, shady patio with a bubble fountain to provide a moist atmosphere is the perfect environment for potted hostas and tree ferns* (Dicksonia antarctica).

PLANTS WITH GOOD FOLIAGE
Ajuga reptans
Aloe
Aucuba
Conifers
Eriobotrya japonica
Ferns
Grasses
Hebe
Hedera
Hosta
Ophiopogon nigrescens
Pulmonaria
Stachys olympica

Architectural Plants

Some plants are grown for their overall impact – usually termed their habit – and they make striking shapes in the garden. If you intend to use the patio mainly in the evening and at night, it is worth including some of these in the planting: they are supremely effective

Above: Melianthus major, *with its luxuriant leaves, stately yuccas and steely blue oat grass add contrasting colour and form to a striking group of foliage plants.*

with subtle lighting, which will highlight large glossy leaves or distinctive silhouettes. Fatsias are usually grown as houseplants, but they are more or less hardy and take kindly to life outdoors in a sheltered spot. Their palm-like, evergreen leaves bring a touch of the exotic to the garden.

Above: Plant Ophiopogon planiscapus 'Nigrescens' *against a light backdrop.*

ARCHITECTURAL PLANTS
FOR PATIOS
Cordyline
Cycas revoluta
Eriobotrya japonica
Fatsia japonica
Mahonia × media
Phormium
Trachycarpus fortunei
Yucca

INTEREST THROUGH THE YEAR

Although patios and terraces receive their heaviest use in summer, when the days are long and you want to spend as much time out of doors as possible, there will usually be odd warm days at other times of the year, and most patios are in full view of the house, so it is well worth making them look attractive all year round.

The garden may be comparatively bare in winter, giving you time to enjoy the design of the patio, but plant life need not be entirely absent from the scene. Some plants flower in winter, and this is, of course, the time when evergreens come into their own.

All bulbs make excellent patio plants. They can be grown in containers but will enjoy the enhanced drainage offered by raised beds. For interest early in the year, try the miniature irises, *Iris danfordiae* and *I. reticulata*, both excellent in shallow pans or troughs. In autumn, the Guernsey lily (*Nerine bowdenii*) or *Amaryllis belladonna* seem to make summer last just that little bit longer.

Clipped evergreens, such as box (*Buxus*), yew (*Taxus*), bay (*Laurus nobilis*) and holly (*Ilex*), provide structure in the garden in winter. If you would rather avoid pruning, try planting any of the dwarf conifers that

Above: *Spring flowers, such as crocuses, primroses and* Iris reticulata, *will add bold splashes of intense colour to the patio early in the year.*

Above: In winter a patio can still be filled with plants: heathers, Viburnum tinus, Euphorbia myrsinites *and a variegated ivy are happy in containers.*

Above: A clipped evergreen, such as this box globe in an elegant metal container, can be used to punctuate the planting at the edge of a patio all year round.

naturally produce a pleasing outline without clipping. *Platycladus* (formerly *Thuja*) *orientalis* 'Aurea Nana' is a distinguished plant, forming a golden egg shape and holding its leaves in stiff, fan-like plates.

If conifers are not to your taste, many of the hebes provide neat mounds of foliage. *Hebe cupressoides* 'Boughton Dome' is a curiosity: it looks like a conifer and, as its name suggests, grows into a perfect dome.

PLANTS FOR WINTER INTEREST
Clematis cirrhosa
*Erica (*winter-flowering forms*)*
*Euonymus (*evergreen*)*
× *Fatshedera lizei*
Hebe
Hedera
*Iris (*winter-flowering forms*)*
Mahonia
Sarcococca
Viola

*Above: The Chusan palm (*Trachycarpus fortunei*) is a dramatic evergreen, best sited where it will be lit by the winter sun.*

Choosing a Style

THERE ARE AS MANY STYLES OF PATIO AS THERE ARE STYLES OF
INDOOR DÉCOR. THIS SECTION EXPLORES JUST A FEW OF THE DESIGN
TRENDS THAT ARE POPULAR TODAY AND SUGGESTS WAYS IN WHICH
THEY CAN BE INTERPRETED ON A PATIO OR TERRACE.

DEFINING STYLE

The decorative aspects of a patio –
from the plants in the borders to the
cushions you place on the garden
chairs – are personal, and what repre-
sents good taste to one gardener may
well be anathema to another.
However, factors such as proportion
and scale are universals. No matter
how you decorate your outdoor space,
a successful patio will be in proportion to the rest of the garden and to
the house, and it should be sympathetic in overall appearance to the
style and materials used for the other
buildings against which it is set.

*Above: Foliage plants clothe the fences
and screen a seat in a restful corner of the
garden, providing dappled shade and
shelter from the breeze.*

Other aspects of design depend on
your approach to life, and it is these
that we tend to think of as embodying
a particular "style". Fashion plays a
part too, and even if you think you are
not a slave to the latest trends, some
become so commonplace that you
can hardly avoid them. Wooden decking is now so widespread and easily
available that it has become the first
choice of many people who would
previously have considered only

Above: Neat metal containers, filled with a phormium, ferns and clipped evergreens, give the garden an orderly air.

Above: These exuberant climbing roses ensure a private and fragrant retreat, even in a town garden.

paving. With a trend as popular as this, however, you need to consider carefully whether it is really the most appropriate material for your garden.

Some people like to give order to their spaces. Others have a more relaxed attitude and may tolerate, even prefer, a certain dishevelment. The two are not mutually exclusive, but a tendency one way or the other may well be evident in how you design and create your garden.

Like the rest of your home, the garden allows you to express your personality. It also reflects the way you choose to spend your time. If you think of the patio as a quiet retreat, you'll plan for privacy and comfort. If your garden is often the setting for parties, your priorities will be space, seating and dramatic lighting effects. If the house opens on to the patio, it is a good idea to relate the two, perhaps

using furniture in similar styles or matching colours. You could extend a tiled floor outside, or echo a wooden floor with decking.

Remember that no scheme need be for ever, and you can change the look with new planting and furniture. Many people update their gardens as often as they change their interiors.

Above: A variety of natural materials can be laid in clean, geometric designs to suit a modern setting.

37

COUNTRY CASUAL

Many town-dwellers would like to bring something of the countryside into their garden, so that it becomes a kind of green lung, with the same function as a park in the middle of a city. The fact that the garden (or a proportion of it) is paved does not prevent this from happening, but a bit more effort may be required to create the desired effect.

Creating the Look

The choice of materials can be critical. Instead of municipal-looking, smooth concrete slabs, look for riven paving in different sizes to create a slightly haphazard look. Decking often looks a little cosmopolitan, especially when the boards are new, but old railway sleepers (ties) have a weathered charm. As far as possible, make sure that the edges of any paved area or raised bed are softened by planting.

When it comes to garden furniture, keep an eye out for wicker or cane chairs, which will have the appropriate rustic character. Weathered pieces of wooden or metal garden furniture can often be found second-hand, and some antique dealers specialize in old garden furniture of high quality – though this can be expensive. For a seaside look, use deck chairs or steamer chairs. A hammock slung between two trees (or possibly between a tree

Above: *A simple arbour made from painted wooden trellis makes a pretty backdrop for plants and an inviting place to sit a while to enjoy the garden.*

Above: Billowing plants in the borders and containers create an exuberant casual effect, disguising the formal shape of a small courtyard garden.

Above: A raised bed provides conditions for plants, such as Zantedeschia aethiopica 'Crowborough', that might not succeed elsewhere in the garden.

and a house wall) makes an idyllic picture in summer and is ideal for a nap on a warm afternoon.

An eclectic mix is appropriate, and *objets trouvés* can provide just the right note. An old metal watering can or that cartwheel will give a hint of rusticity. If you cannot find old terracotta pots, paint new ones with sour milk or yoghurt to encourage mosses and lichens to take a hold.

Planting

A cottage garden is primarily one of early and high summer. Typical flowers include all kinds of roses, especially the scented ones, old-fashioned pinks (*Dianthus*) and a host of annuals. Pelargoniums are cheerful and bright and will flower for months. Lavender (*Lavandula*) is an excellent low-grow-

ing hedging plant and will provide a romantic haze of colour when in flower (as well as attracting swarms of bees).

Aim for a riotous mix of colour and don't forget the fruit and vegetables without which no true cottage gardener could survive for long.

Above: A pot overflowing with herbs epitomizes the cottage garden style.

MODERN

If you have a beautiful, architect-designed house and are a naturally neat and tidy person with an uncluttered lifestyle, this may well be the look for you.

Creating the Look

Absolutely up-to-date materials are *de rigueur* for high-tech designers, and metals and plastics are likely to be used as often as more traditional materials. Inventive finishes are important: marble and granite, for instance – surely the most desirable of all traditional building materials – can be polished to a glass-like surface or given a more frosted appearance. Crushed CDs, a recent innovation to be used in place of gravel and crushed shells, have a real sparkle.

A smart urban look can be created using a limited colour palette, in both materials and plants. While natural materials are generally left to speak for themselves, artificial ones are often dyed to shades that would never occur in nature. You can find manmade pebbles in bright blues and reds and plastic pots in a range of colours.

If you have a keen design sense (or are able to employ a designer), you might like to experiment with asymmetric shapes, but make sure that the design is not too dominant. Look beyond gardening for your inspiration: architectural magazines and the world of industry and product design may well ignite your creative fire.

A possible drawback is that a garden in this style can date quickly as new trends emerge.

Above: *Smooth tiles and mirrors create an illusion of space on a small modern terrace.*

Above: Top-dressing pots with some of the cobbles that have been used for the patio surface will help give coherence to the overall design.

Above: Colour can be used on both boundaries and containers to create a sense of unity. Even the spiral plant supports are blue.

Planting

On the green front, stick to plants that have a strong outline and architectural form. Spiky succulents, such as agaves, are perfect but will not tolerate extremes of cold and wet. Phormiums and the Chusan palm (*Trachycarpus fortunei*) are hardier and just as dramatic.

Low-growing plants with metallic-looking leaves include *Houttuynia cordata* and *Ajuga reptans* 'Burgundy Glow'. Selected forms of *Pulmonaria saccharata* Argentea Group have interestingly marbled leaves, and *Heuchera* 'Pewter Moon' makes satisfying clumps of silver-grey foliage. Many grasses are perfect for the modern look,

and they can be used on their own, either planted *en masse* or displayed for effect in matching containers.

Most flowers do not really belong in a garden of this type, but they need not be eliminated entirely, and those with a sculptural form are best. Spring-flowering hyacinths have a stiff habit and their thick, glossy leaves look positively unreal. Planted in quantity, they look (and smell) sensational. For summer interest, grow lilies, with their trumpet-like flowers. *Zantedeschia aethiopica* is a plant of unsurpassed elegance, with cool-looking, heart-shaped leaves and smooth-textured, white, arum-type flowers. It is perfect near (or even in) water.

MEDITERRANEAN

Memories of Mediterranean summers make many of us long for lazy days of outdoor living, soaking up the sun or relaxing in leafy shade, surrounded by the scents of aromatic herbs, pines and citrus. A real Mediterranean garden is usually a shady place, often a courtyard, brightened with pots of vivid flowers and sheltered by a pergola draped with fruiting vines. Walls and woodwork, often bleached and cracked by the sun, are painted in the Mediterranean palette of clear blues, dusky pinks, terracotta or white.

Above: Pale decking reflects the available light and large terracotta containers give a strongly Mediterranean feel.

Creating the Look

In cooler climates, a Mediterranean-style patio can maximize the available sunshine by using white or pale paving to reflect heat on to the plants. Another way to achieve this is through the use of gravel or, if your budget will stretch to it, dolomite chippings. If you can lay out the garden as a series of terraces that face the sun, so much the better. A brick or stone wall that faces the sun will retain the day's heat and radiate it at dusk, appreciably raising the ambient temperature. To a lesser degree, so will stone and terracotta pots and paving.

Your Mediterranean patio should include a shaded area to offer relief from the sun on the hottest days. Erect a simple pergola over a seat or table, and plant climbers to scramble over it.

A positive aspect of this style is that you will feel as if you are always on holiday – at least as long as the sun is shining. As soon as wet weather arrives, you may notice that gravel starts to turn green as moss and lichens take hold. Either chemical treatments or a blast with a pressure washer will solve this problem for you.

Planting

Typical plants of the Mediterranean include most of the woody herbs, including thyme, rosemary and lavender, which thrive in gritty, well-drained soil in your sunniest spot. These,

together with rock roses (*Cistus* and *Helianthemum*), with gummy, aromatic stems, will fill the patio with evocative scents as well as attracting bees and butterflies. Oleanders (*Nerium oleander*) are also characteristic of the region, with their leathery leaves and richly coloured flowers (but they are poisonous, so treat them with care). Pelargoniums flower all summer, giving bold splashes of white, pink and red. If you need an accent plant, a fig, olive or citrus tree would be perfect.

Most of these plants respond well to being grown in containers or raised beds, making them ideal patio plants.

Mediterranean plants do not take kindly to long periods of cold, wet weather, though they will survive lower temperatures if planted in open, gritty soil. You can move delicate subjects in pots under cover in winter.

Above: Brightly painted furniture and accessories, with flowers in strong, warm colours, create a Mediterranean feel in a sunny corner of this patio.

*Above: Evergreen bay (*Laurus nobilis*) grows readily in a container and is easily clipped into decorative shapes.*

43

Above: A sheltered corner of the patio takes on a jungly character when lavishly filled with foliage plants. Although they look exotic, they are all quite hardy.

HOT AND EXOTIC

Surprisingly, it is not actually necessary to live in a hot climate to create a tropical look in your garden, and the enclosed, sheltered conditions found on many patios, which may have protecting walls on two and even three sides, often provide the ideal micro-climate for many exotic plants that would not otherwise survive.

Creating the Look

The keynote to success is to include lots of foliage plants, preferably the large-leaved kind. If you have enough greenery you will actually increase the humidity level of the garden, creating the jungle-like environment in which these plants will thrive. Bearing in mind that a lot of tropical plants have

adapted to low light levels, this style can be an effective design solution to a predominantly shady site.

A timber deck creates the appropriate colonial atmosphere, and the furnishings might be either huge wicker chairs or teak recliners. A mosquito net would provide a witty reference to the tropics, especially if there were a pool nearby.

Planting

Huge bamboos actually look extremely effective in a confined space and are hardy. Try also banana palms (*Musa basjoo*), which will require some winter protection. If the patio is shaded, you may prefer a tree fern (*Dicksonia antarctica*). Buy the biggest you can afford, because they grow at a rate of only 2.5cm (1in) a year, so if you buy

Above: Small pans of succulents will enjoy the warmth reflected from the paving.

a youngster you will have to be prepared for a long wait. Large specimens are expensive but worth the outlay when you consider the drama they bring to a garden.

Above: Succulents in pots, which do duty as houseplants, will benefit from being moved outside in summer.

An interesting and less often seen alternative is the loquat (*Eriobotrya japonica*). In a cold climate it is hardly likely to fruit, but you can enjoy it for its exotic-looking, long, pleated leaves.

Remember that if you have a lot of houseplants you can move them outdoors in summer (when there is no risk of night frosts) to enhance the tropical atmosphere.

A Desert Patio

If your patio is really hot and exposed, a desert-style planting scheme might be appropriate, concentrating on cacti and succulents. Some cacti are surprisingly tolerant of cold. What they hate is damp, muggy weather, which causes rotting, so good drainage is vital.

They will thrive in gravel beds, which can be given extra structure by the addition of rocks or pebbles.

In this kind of garden you need to avoid any suspicion of lushness. Smooth-rendered walls will enhance the desert feel and reflect sunlight and heat on to the plants, staying warm even as the temperature drops in the evening. Leave gaps for the plants among paving stones, or make larger beds by laying a weed-suppressing membrane over the soil and planting through it before topping with gravel or cobbles. On a smaller scale, fill troughs or planters with succulents.

It is possible to replicate this look even in a cold climate if you keep your exotic plants in pots for enjoying indoors in winter. Plunge them into their beds in the summer.

ORIENTAL

The Zen principles on which the classic gardens of Japan and China are laid out probably baffle most Westerners, but this is no reason why we should not borrow some of the ideas to create Oriental-style gardens that are places of peace and tranquillity and conducive to contemplation.

Creating the Look

The true Japanese garden usually contains only a few plants. Everything depends on the balance of a few elements: rocks, raked gravel, water and maybe a conifer or Japanese maple (*Acer*). Any tree with an interesting outline will do, however. In essence,

Above: Low, clean lines using natural materials, and the restrained use of foliage plants, create an elegant, structured look that echoes Japanese garden design.

Above: Topiarized box, trained into the traditional cloud form, is a feature of Oriental-style gardens.

the style is rather akin to the minimalist garden and will suit anyone who does not have a great deal of time on their hands, since what plants there are need little maintenance. The style also lends itself to a shady site.

Alternatively, you might like to borrow some elements of feng shui. Although this philosophy is more often thought of in relation to interior design, the principles are equally applicable outdoors. You may want to incorporate wind chimes (but think of your neighbours, who might be profoundly irritated by the tinkling sound that you find so charming) and a water feature, but it is how you place them in relation to each other that counts. Any paths should be winding, to symbolize the winding route of life.

Planting

China is often referred to as the mother of all gardens, because a huge number of the plants that are now most prized in cultivation originated there. There is therefore no shortage of plant material available to help you create an Oriental look: whether you prefer blowsy peonies or delicate grasses, you will be able to find the appropriate species.

The classic Japanese garden is predominantly green, imitating a natural landscape. Japanese maples (*Acer japonicum* and *A. palmatum*) have an elegant habit that you can enhance by wiring the stems as they grow to create an authentic gnarled appearance.

Velvety, vivid green moss is essential to the look. You can encourage it to colonize rocks by painting their shady sides with sour milk or yoghurt, but keep walkways and steps clear of moss as it can be very slippery.

If you must have flowers, some of the China roses, such as *Rosa* 'Cécile Brünner', are delightfully dainty, and many of the so-called patio roses seem to owe much to their Chinese forebears, making them ideal for an Oriental garden. Oriental lilies and chrysanthemums, such as 'Emperor of China', could complete the picture.

On a tiny patio, you might like to include some bonsai in Oriental pots.

Above: This serene Buddha would make the perfect finishing touch to an Oriental-style patio.

Above: Dainty but floriferous, Rosa 'Cécile Brünner' is ideal for a large container in a Chinese-style garden.

Special Features

ONCE THE PATIO IS BUILT, FINISHING TOUCHES WILL HELP TO BRING IT TO LIFE. A CAREFULLY PLACED POT, AN UNUSUAL SCULPTURE OR INTRIGUING ITEMS OF FURNITURE CAN PROVIDE THE ACCENTS OF COLOUR AND SHAPE NEEDED TO TIE THE WHOLE SCHEME TOGETHER.

CONTAINERS

Any area of hard landscaping can be enlivened by plants in pots, and if your garden consists of nothing other than a paved area, as is often the case with courtyard gardens, containers provide your only chance of introducing greenery.

Types of Container

For an integrated look, match the container to materials used in the patio or to the style you are trying to create.

Terracotta pots are valued by nearly all gardeners for their unobtrusive character: they never detract from the

Above: The subtle patina of this metal container is well set off by the paving stones and the cool planting of white tulips and delicate purple violets.

Above: Introduce some Mediterranean colour by painting terracotta pots in a range of clear greens and blues.

plant and usually enhance it. Use them freely in a Mediterranean or cottage garden. If necessary, they can be painted with plant-friendly, water-based paints to match furniture or other features. Painting them white can help brighten a dark, gloomy corner.

Synthetic materials are often used to imitate more expensive natural ones, such as lead and terracotta, but some plastic pots unashamedly proclaim what they are. They can work well on a patio designed in a modernist style, but will need replacing as they fade or crack in sunlight. Galvanized containers look particularly good in a modern setting, while copper and bronze develop beautiful patinas as they age.

Glazed terracotta pots, often in jewel-like colours, suit a colonial or Oriental-style patio and look good with decking. Versailles planters – handsome wooden cases designed to conceal a pot inside – are ideal for clipped or topiarized evergreens and can be painted in any colour.

Plants for Containers

Bulbs for spring interest, later replaced by summer bedding plants, are traditional choices for containers, but a huge range of other plants will thrive in pots. If they are to occupy a prominent position on the patio or terrace, the most valuable plants are those with a long season of interest.

All dwarf conifers can be grown successfully in containers. Slow-growing evergreens such as hollies (*Ilex*), box (*Buxus*) and spotted laurel (*Aucuba japonica* 'Crotonifolia') are also excellent.

If you want flowering shrubs, camellias are ideal. They respond well to pruning and their glossy foliage is always attractive. Growing in pots allows you to use tender shrubs, such as abutilon and oleander, which must be moved inside for winter protection.

Many edible crops can be grown in containers. Leafy salad crops and dwarf beans are ideal patio vegetables,

cut-and-come again lettuces being particularly successful. Tomatoes, a traditional patio plant, can be grown in large containers. In a warm area, you could also try bell peppers, chilli peppers and aubergines (eggplant).

Fruit can also be grown in containers. Apple trees on dwarfing rootstocks are ideal for a sheltered patio. A potted fig is a delight, but in a cold area you will need to train the branches across a warm wall for good fruiting. Olives and citruses are beautiful container plants, and this is a sensible way to grow them as they are not reliably hardy, so need protection in a conservatory or greenhouse in winter.

It makes sense to grow culinary herbs close to the kitchen, and a group of containers filled with fragrant mint, sage, thyme and rosemary will delight the senses as well as being conveniently sited for alfresco eating.

Above: *Easy to cultivate and very attractive when grown in a container, strawberries are the perfect patio fruit.*

49

Above: An old chimney pot offers a cool root run for clematis, and additional shade is provided by the other plants.

CARING FOR PLANTS IN POTS

Plants in containers need a little more care and attention than those grown in the open garden.

Choosing a Planting Medium

For a seasonal planting, multi-purpose potting mixes are excellent. For permanent and long-term plantings, soil-based products usually give better results because they are more water retentive. They are also heavier and thus give the container greater stability. Ericaceous (acid) potting mix can be used if you are planting lime-hating plants such as camellias, rhododendrons and heathers.

For plants that need good drainage, such as lavender, rosemary and artemisia, replace up to one-third of

the mix with horticultural grit or perlite. This is especially important with plants of borderline hardiness.

Feeding and Watering

All containers need regular watering when the plants are in active growth (usually from spring to autumn) to prevent the potting mix from drying out. Drench the containers thoroughly at each watering. If you can deliver the water as a fine spray, so much the better: a jet can compact the surface, preventing the water from penetrating to the roots. At the height of summer you may need to water twice a day or even more.

For a seasonal display, especially if you are growing annuals in window-boxes and hanging baskets, you can minimize the risk of the plants drying out by adding some water-retaining

PERMANENT PLANTS
FOR CONTAINERS

Acacia
Acer
Aucuba
Buxus
Camellia
Clematis
Conifers
Cordyline
Hedera
Herbs
Ilex
Laurus nobilis
Olea
Rhododendron
Rosa (patio cultivars)

crystals to the potting mix at planting time, but you will still need to water at regular intervals.

All plants grown in containers benefit from feeding, since the nutrients present in the potting mix are soon used up by the plants. Look for flowering plant fertilizers or a tomato feed, both of which are high in potassium to trigger good flowering and fruiting. Organic products, which are often based on seaweed, are becoming more widely available.

Always follow the manufacturer's recommendations on rates of application. A single dose of some fertilizers will feed for a whole season, while others must be repeated at regular intervals. Slow-release fertilizer pellets can be added to summer containers but they are not suitable for permanent planting.

Winter Care

Plants in containers are especially vulnerable in cold weather because the roots, which are above ground level, can easily be frozen, especially if excess water cannot drain quickly away from the potting mix. If frosts are threatened, protect pots by wrapping them loosely in sacking or some other air-permeable material. You can keep frost off developing flowerbuds (on early camellias, for example) by tenting the top growth loosely in some horticultural fleece.

PLANTS FOR SUMMER CONTAINERS
Begonia
Bidens
Fuchsia
Lobelia
Osteospermum
Pelargonium
Petunia
Tropaeolum
Verbena

FOOD PLANTS FOR CONTAINERS
Apples (on dwarf rooting stocks)
Aubergines (eggplants)
Beetroots
Bell peppers
Citrus
Figs
French beans
Spinach beet
Strawberries
Tomatoes

Above: A patio near the kitchen is ideal for herbs and vegetables, and you will notice immediately if they need watering.

51

FURNITURE

The range of garden furniture available today is wide, and you can choose the type best suited to your needs. You need to consider, for instance, if the furniture is to stand outdoors all year round or if you are going to store it under cover, in the garage or garden shed, when not in use. Not all garden furniture is designed for comfort, so you may want to invest in a few cushions.

Different furniture fulfils different purposes. A steamer chair is perfect for lolling in the sun with a refreshing drink and the Sunday newspaper but is less than ideal if you are eating a formal meal. If you are planning a barbecue, you might like to dispense with seating altogether, to encourage guests to mingle more freely. The edges of raised beds or a raised pool can make good improvised seating if they are deep and secure enough.

A few large cushions scattered on a deck will look inviting. Neutral colours – pale cream, beige and grey – usually work better than bright colours and busy patterns (especially those with flowers), which can detract from the pleasures of the living garden.

Heavy furniture, such as cast iron and stone, is attractive but difficult to move once it is in place. If your patio is small and has to accommodate different activities at different times, lightweight alternatives are more convenient. A table need not be a permanent feature of the patio, and the most basic folding table looks attractive when covered with a tablecloth.

Above: A simple garden bench and fragrant flowers are all that is needed to make a delightful sanctuary.

Above: These dainty metal chairs are surprisingly comfortable and make an ideal choice for a small area, as they are in keeping with its scale.

Above: These two throne-like chairs on a raised terrace echo the curves of the patio design and have been used as its most dominant feature.

Types of Furniture

Top of the range is cast-iron furniture, which is expensive and heavy and is, in consequence, no longer made in great quantities. Antique pieces are extremely sought after and are usually highly decorative. Aluminium reproductions are much cheaper and lighter but are not always entirely convincing. Wire furniture, often painted white but more often these days coated in plastic, is highly ornate and perhaps best suited to a Victorian-style conservatory, although it is light enough to carry on to the patio in warm weather.

Wooden furniture is also expensive, especially if it is made of teak (the best wood for the purpose), but it is a sound investment and ages sympathetically. It will need treating with teak oil from time to time to stop the wood drying out and cracking. You should make sure that any teak furniture you buy is certified as having been made of wood from a sustainable source.

Deck chairs and director's chairs are convenient because they can be folded up and stored flat when they are not in use. They are also light enough to be moved from place to place as needed.

Bamboo, cane and rattan furniture is ideal for creating a colonial look, but it is not especially weatherproof. A coat of varnish can help prevent cracking, but this type of furniture is seldom long-lived.

Plastic furniture is usually cheap and readily available, but you may need to shop around to find a range that is really sympathetic. On the plus side, it is lightweight and can be painted or otherwise customized with cushions made to fit. Pre-formed plastic chairs are often stackable, which makes winter storage easy.

WATER FEATURES

A pool or fountain will add life to the patio, in more ways than one. Not only is the sound of water reviving – most people find it soothing, particularly in the evening – but water will attract a range of fauna into the garden: frogs, toads and newts as well as a host of insects.

Types of Water Feature

A patio or deck that meets or overhangs a pool looks dramatic, while even a small pool set into the paving or decking brings all the pleasures of a pool in the open garden. Formal, geometric pools work best close to a house, and they should ideally be based on the proportions of the house windows or doors and built with the same type of materials as the house.

Remember that it will be difficult (if not impossible) to excavate for a sunken pool on an existing patio. If you are building your patio from scratch and would like to include a pool, allow for the depth of the water in the height of the patio. The alternative is to build a raised pool surrounded by paving, a wooden framework or railway sleepers (ties).

If you favour an expanse of still water, try to site the pool away from trees, as leaves will rot and pollute the water. Most surface-growing water plants do best in sun, but if the pool is purely ornamental a shaded site is permissible, and you can keep the water clear with a chemical cleansing agent.

On a large patio a fountain would be the ultimate luxury, especially in a hot, dry climate. Cascades can be

Above: A well-planted raised pool is ideal on a patio because it does not involve excavating below the hard surface.

Above: When running, the wall-mounted spout will be a focal point and provide the refreshing sound of trickling water.

impressive, but for a really imposing fall of water a large reservoir and powerful submersible pump are needed. If you have a small pool in a sunny position and would like a fountain, look for one that is solar-powered. These are becoming more widely available and more attractive. Some models have separate solar panels, but increasingly they are manufactured with integral panels.

If you have small children most kinds of water feature are best avoided altogether: it is possible to drown in even the shallowest water. Installing a bubble fountain can be a good compromise because no deep water is accessible, but remember that the reservoir and pump must be housed below ground level and hidden by cobbles that sit on top of a mesh. Such

Above: A keen sense of humour is evident in the design of this water spout in a wooden half-barrel. Small raised features like this are quite simple to install.

features involve excavating below the level of the patio, so this must be taken into account during the planning process.

Many styles of ready-made water feature are available from garden suppliers, and these are simple to install. Designs such as a brimming urn or village pump are popular, and if ground space is really restricted, a wall spout that feeds into a basin just below can be delightful. Wall-mounted water features should never be fitted directly to a house wall, and it may be necessary to erect a double wall to house the pipe and pump.

Introducing the electricity needed to power a submersible pump should be considered during the planning stages. Because water and electricity are a lethal combination, seek professional advice about the appropriate switches and cables.

Above: If you choose a water feature that relies on a circulating pump, make sure you can excavate below ground for the sump.

LIGHTING

You will get the most use from your patio or terrace on summer evenings if you add some form of lighting. If the patio is some distance from the house but is visible from it, lighting it can bring an element of drama that you can also enjoy from the comfort of indoors at other seasons. Imagine the effect of floodlighting when the ground is covered in snow.

All electrical lighting systems powered from the mains should be installed by a qualified electrician. Regulations stipulate how deep electric cables should be buried, and these should be adhered to. As with cabling for a pool, the lighting cables should be laid before the patio or terrace is built, but if this is not possible they should be buried where no digging that could damage the wires is likely to take place.

Remember that outdoor lighting should be designed to be seen only within your own garden. Your neighbours may prefer their gardens to be dark at night.

Types of Lighting

The simplest way to illuminate your patio is with candles or flares. Obviously, these are not permanent, and they must be supervised at all times. Both are best in still weather, but flares are much less likely to blow out than candles; you will need to

Above: *This brass oil or paraffin lamp is easily portable and looks beautiful whether it is lit or not.*

ensure that they can be properly supported in the ground or in stable containers. Candles can be housed in lanterns and distributed around the patio or suspended from trees.

Low-voltage lighting is cheap but is best used to edge a path, since the light shed will not be particularly strong. For safety, paths should always be lit at night if the garden is going to be used then, and solar-powered lights are now available that are ideal for this purpose.

Floodlights are much more powerful, and many dramatic effects can be achieved if they are sited with care. If

Above: Dramatic uplighting from the patio gives this delicate maple an added attraction at night.

there is a tree overhanging the patio, it is a charming idea to festoon it with fairy lights (coloured or not) or individual lanterns.

Underwater lamps can be used to light up a pond and will keep any fish active until well into the evening.

HEATING

Various forms of heating are available to bring a touch of warmth to those evenings when there is a chill in the air after sundown.

Perhaps the cosiest is the chiminea, a Mexican stove, which is open at the front and the top and is usually made of terracotta. These are designed as wood-burners, but you will need to substitute a non-smoking fuel if you live in a smokeless zone. They are made in a range of sizes. They need to be supervised at all times when lit and can pose a hazard if there are small children around.

Gas patio heaters are surprisingly stylish. They are usually fed by bottled gas rather than connected to the mains supply and are lit at the top, the heat being deflected downwards by a small canopy. They can look rather like municipal street lamps, but on a cool autumn evening the warmth they emit will be welcome.

Above: Lighting a water feature brings drama to the patio after sundown.

SAFETY FIRST

Be sure to keep a fire extinguisher handy at all times if you are lighting or heating your patio with any form of naked flame.

MIRRORS

Not everyone appreciates the use of mirrors in a garden. There is no doubt that they increase the sense of size of a small space, but some people are unnerved by catching a glimpse of themselves. There is also the argument that birds will fly into them, although this is unlikely in an enclosed space such as a patio or terrace, since most birds prefer to keep to the trees if there is no clear runway for take-off.

If you include a mirror, site it with care for maximum impact, angling it slightly so that visitors to the garden do not merely see their own reflections. Placed at the end of a path, it will make the garden seem endless. If you have no paths, put a mirror where it will reflect a particular feature: a statue, a large container or even just a garden door. Mirrors are especially effective in association with water features, but they must be set perfectly upright if distorting effects are to be avoided. Disguise the mirror's presence by surrounding it with planting to hide the edges.

Use mirrors designed for outdoor use; those made for indoors are not particularly weatherproof and will soon begin to deteriorate.

ORNAMENTS

A well-chosen ornament can bring a touch of distinction to a patio, especially in winter when there may be a shortage of plant material to bring the

Above: *An unusual metallic trellis functions as a mirror, creating the illusion that the garden is more colourful than it actually is.*

Above: *An arbour festooned with flowers makes a frame for a piece of classical statuary, creating a theatrical effect.*

area to life. They can be given a position of some prominence or be hidden among plants or pots to make a personal or witty reference. Reflected in water or a mirror, their impact will be doubled. At best, they give a sense of permanence to the garden.

Make sure the ornament is in scale, but err on the large side if you are in doubt. Too small an ornament will look mean and lost, but one that is large will look grand and imposing and will make a considerable impact on a small patio.

Types of Ornament

Garden statuary is a matter of taste. Top of the list would be a work (possibly abstract) from a sculptor's studio, but this is likely to be beyond the purse and aspirations of most gardeners. Garden centres stock a wide range of mass-produced ornaments, and whether your preference is for stone animals or abstract designs such as obelisks or balls, you will probably find something to suit your patio.

For something a little more individual, go to a reclamation yard, where you can often find old statues and other ornaments. A rusted piece of agricultural equipment can make an appealing *objet trouvé*. Ceramics can be beautiful, though the production process limits their size. If you are naturally creative, you could try making your own abstract piece.

Above: The face of a cherub, in reflective mood, peers through the ivy, adding a charming touch to the eaves of this garden shed.

Materials

Bronze is beautiful and ages sympathetically, but the price is likely to be prohibitive. Nowadays, synthetic resins provide a convincing substitute at a much lower cost. Stone ornaments are heavy, and reconstituted stone pieces often have a tell-tale seam left from the mould that betrays their manufacture. However, they weather beautifully, acquiring an attractive covering of moss in time.

Plastic ornaments are light and tend to blow over, so they are perhaps best used among plants rather than as stand-alone features. Ceramics need to be securely placed, since they can crack or even break if they fall over.

59

AWNINGS AND SHADE

If the patio catches the midday sun you may find the glare and heat all but unbearable in summer. If there is no tree nearby, an awning or overhead screen can cast the necessary shade.

Types of Awning

Some awnings are designed to be attached to a house wall and are operated either manually or electronically. This restricts both their use and their design: they are an option only if the patio abuts a house wall; there must be a sufficient stretch of wall to accommodate them, and they must be rectangular or square in shape. If placed just above a sitting-room window or a pair of patio doors, they will

Above: *A bespoke awning over a patio can make a bold design statement.*

have the dual function of shading the room. This type of awning is traditionally made of striped fabric with a scalloped or fringed edge. If you want something a little more individual, you could have a bespoke canopy made of canvas or sailcloth, to sling between poles or the patio walls.

If the patio is some distance from a suitable wall, a stand-alone awning will be required. At its simplest, this could be a large parasol; these are often designed to be used in conjunction with a table, and they have the advantage that they can be moved around as the direction of the sun changes. A rectangular gazebo, like a tent with open sides, will keep sun or rain off a larger table and chairs.

No awning is fully weatherproof. If accidentally left in the rain, they should be allowed to dry out fully then stored dry under cover.

Pergolas and Arbours

If you are building a completely new patio that is likely to be in full sun for most of the day, consider building a pergola to provide shade over part of it. A pergola is simply a framework of wooden posts with cross-pieces, but when it is clothed with climbing plants in summer it can become a shady room. A free-standing pergola constructed some distance from the house and built over a paved area will be a private, shady place.

A well-built pergola will be strong enough to support a large wisteria or fruiting vine, but it is also a perfect structure over which honeysuckle, roses and clematis can be trained. The deciduous hop (*Humulus lupulus*) will provide reliable summer shade but disappear in winter to admit all the available light.

An arbour is smaller in scale than a pergola but also offers opportunities to create a hideaway covered with fragrant climbers. Even a simple rustic arch, set against a hedge, will provide sufficient shelter for a table and two chairs, and a larger area, perhaps with a gazebo or summerhouse, will be a delightful retreat on a hot day.

Above: On a small patio, a focal point can be created at ground level by using surface materials creatively.

CREATING A FOCAL POINT

A focal point is an important aspect of any garden design, providing a resting place for the eye in much the same way as a fireplace in a sitting room, even though there may be other objects of interest present.

It need not be a permanent fixture. If, for instance, your patio is some distance from the house but visible from it, a well-positioned chair might be used to draw your attention to it.

A more permanent focal point can be provided by an ornament, a large container or an imposing plant, and other elements on the patio can be arranged to lead the eye toward it. A series of linked focal points can be useful in a large garden to draw different elements together, but they should be positioned so that they are not all visible simultaneously. Only when you arrive at one focal point will you be aware of the presence of another. Conversely, a single object can do double duty at the axis of two paths, providing the focal point for both. There is no limit to the number of visual games you can play.

Mark out the position of focal points with string stretched between pegs, and move them around until you find the right spot for the object. If the intended focal point already exists – for instance a garden door or a tree – use the string to determine the lie of the paths.

Acknowledgments

Gardens and Designers
p5: Wendy and Michael Perry, Bosvigo House, Truro, Cornwall.
p6 below: 'Mr McGregor's Garden'/designer: Jacqui Gordon, RHS Chelsea Flower Show 1999.
p7: Designer: Declan Buckley and Bernard Hickie (dbdesign@dircon.co.uk and bernardhickie@mac.com).
p8: Fovant hut, Wiltshire/designer: Christina Oates.
p10, 15 and 46b: National Garden Exhibition Centre 2001.
p16 and 60: Trevyn McDowell's garden/designer: Paul Thompson.
p18, 28 and 54ta: Peter Robinson's garden, Suffolk.
p19a: RHS Tatton Park Flower Show, 2001.
p20a: East Ruston Old Vicarage, Norfolk/designer: Alan Gray and Graham Robeson.
p20b: RHS Chelsea Flower Show 1999.
p21: Bill and Amanda Alexander, Crouch Hill/designer: Lucy Summers.
p23l: National Garden Exhibition Centre 2001.
p23r and 33b: Renée Lynch's garden/designer: Sally Court.
p24 and 56: Mrs Winkle-Howarth (owner and designer), London.
p33a and 47l: Gerald Kite's garden/designer: Declan Buckley. Hard landscaping by Robert Kite (Kitescape, 020 7738 6512).
p37l: RIBA café garden, London/designer: Elsie Josland.
p41r: RHS Chelsea Flower Show 2001.
p42: Hannah Peshar Sculpture Gallery, Black and White Cottage, Ockley, Surrey; deck designed by Antony Paul, stoneware by Jennifer Jones.
p44a: Charlotte Gross's garden/designer: Declan Buckley.

Above: Allowing plants to colonize hard landscaping creates interest.

p53r: 'The Princess and the Frog'/designer: Shari Lawrence Garden Design, RHS Hampton Court Flower Show 2001.
p55b: Steel water feature designed by Ben Pike.
p55r: Designer: Susan Sharkey/Sculptor: Dennis Fairweather.
p57 both: Sumil Wicke's garden/designer: Lara Copley-Smith

Photographers
Peter Anderson: 18, 26, 28, 32, 35b, 41r, 45, 47r, 51, 54l, 58l, 64.
Jonathan Buckley: 20both, 25, 29, 30, 35tal, 39ar, 55r.
Sarah Cuttle: 55l.
John Freeman: 4, 13, 15a, 22, 27, 34, 36, 37b, 39tl, 40, 44b, 50, 52.
Andrea Jones: 11bl, 39b.
Simon McBride: 9ar, 14br, 19b, 29r, 33b, 43, 53l, 54r.
Marie O'Hara: 12.
Debbie Patterson: 6t, 14br, 37ar, 38, 58r, 50.
Jo Whitworth: 6b, 8, 35ar, 41l, 42, 55r.
Steve Wooster: 5, 7, 9al, 10, 11br, 15b, 16, 17, 19a, 20a, 21, 23, 24, 31, 33, 37al, 44a, 46, 47l, 51r, 53r, 56, 57, 60, 61.

Index

Index

Above: This parterre-like patio combines tiles with formally clipped box.

PERFECT
PATIOS
& TERRACES

Discover the pleasure and versatility of a well-planned
courtyard to enjoy day or night

•

Ideas for designing an outdoor room for different functions,
from entertaining guests to relaxing

•

Create a harmonious effect with furniture, plants and
special features that complement each other

•

Enjoy a miniature garden that appeals to the senses of
sight, sound, touch, taste and smell

Andrew Mikolajski is a highly regarded
horticultural expert and gardening
author. In his writing he combines
his technical knowledge of plants
with practical experience of creating
his own country garden.

ISBN 1-84215

9 781842 156889

Printed in China